Writing Down the Words

Writing Down
the Words

Selected Poems by
Dan Carleton

Copyright © 2022 Daniel Webster Carleton
ggearinc@yahoo.com
www.geargearinc.com

ISBN 978-0-578-36260-1

Library of Congress Control Number: 2021924367

Published in Detroit, Michigan, United States of America

First Printing, 2022

Thanks to Diane Fead for the illustrations
Thanks to Shelley Seccombe for the photographs

To all of my grandchildren, even the unborn

Contents

Acknowledgments

I am grateful to all who taught me and influenced me as a writer, but won't attempt to list people, except a few dead ones. Nuel P Davis, Otis Kidwell Burger, Bill Merwin, and my favorite poet: Dylan Thomas.

Introduction

Encouraged by my mother, I started writing poetry (at least she called it that) when I was eight years old.

Poetry is a hard master. Whether I was feeling good, bad, lonely, stupid or indignant it wouldn't let me alone. Although none of those early efforts still exist in their original form, many of the thoughts and feelings and objects have made it into this volume. Lobsters, boats, cars, comets and above all people reside herein, and I apologize to all that I have damaged by including or by excluding them.

During my time at University of Illinois as a student and later a teacher I tried to get away from poetry. As a student of Psychology, Biology and later Art; but once I managed to graduate I got stuck as a graduate assistant teaching—you guessed it, Poetry. As a graduate student I had the privilege to arrange poetry readings for the English Department, and thus got acquainted with some of the greats of the 60s and '70s. W.S. Merwin, William Stafford and Philip Booth were just a few of the poets I was privileged to meet and show around the lovely old Champaign Urbana campus; and best of all, I got to attend the readings as an usher/chaperone/and general dogsbody to some great poets.

I was never intent on publishing my stuff. I am far too critical to do so easily; but now as I approach my seventh decade of writing the stuff, I finally feel the need to put it in book form to leave to friends and family.

Most of my family somehow wound up in the arts: writing or publishing books, articles, songs, photographs or music. I have included a few of my father's poems, which he wrote after serving in Europe in WWI. I did not know he had written anything but books on plants until I found a bunch of his non-scientific writing after he died. But I owe much to the sound of his old manual Underwood banging away in his basement office.

Perhaps it gave me some of my consciousness of rhythm. Not to pass over Mom, who wrote music and studied in Paris in the early

20th century with Nadia Boulanger. She beat her children into studying music. Shelley the violin, Nancy her lovely voice, and me the 'cello.

But other poets have always been my teachers. If I had to pick one poet's work to take to prison or a desert island it would be Dylan Thomas, but there are so many I refuse to name them. My sister Shelley introduced me to one of her New York friends, Otis Kidwell Burger (see my elegy poem to Otis in the book) who challenged me to write outside my comfort zone. Thus, the title of this book and the first poem of the collection came from her encouragement to step outside.

Finally, a few words about rules: I hate them, but here are mine: The rules of poetry
  1) There are no rules for writing poetry.
  2) A title is more powerful than most lines.
  3) Repeat words and phrases for emphasis.
  4) Take advantage of opportunities to create double meanings.
  5) Punctuation has meaning, full stop.
  6) Read yours aloud to yourself, rhythm is critical.
  7) Read lots of other poets
  8) If these rules seem good to you, see rule number 1.

10/26/2021

Writing Down the Words

Writing Down the Words

Step
    By
      Step
        By
          Step
Like your feet walking
Walking like your feet are
Approaching a goal, any goal.
Your feet, perhaps dactylic feet
Approaching a goal, perhaps a poem
Perhaps approaching a lover, hesitant feet
Inch by inch, foot by foot, and meter by meter.
Meter maybe Iambic, Trochaic Spondaic, Anapestic
But my favorite is the Pyrrhic neither syllable stressed
Stressless is my choice for the rhythm of our lives.
The meter of my walking is not very important
What has the feel of importance is the goal
The writing down of words is the goal
Writing the words the end itself
Words will become a poem
Writing is like walking
        Step
      By
    Step
  By
Step

03/08/2021

My Last Poem

This could be my last poem.
It could be, might be
My last
The virus lurks outside my door
Waiting for admission
Waiting for permission to come in,
Waiting

The virus has a name: Living
And this poem has a name: My Last
So I refuse to write it.
Cannot write it.
Will not write it.
It is waiting
For permission to be written
Waiting

I emphatically refuse to write my last poem.
It may insist on being written.
It may stomp an iambic or dactylic foot outside the door
But to hell with it.
Poems have to come from somewhere and
This one is still waiting outside the door:
Waiting.

Let it wait.

12/23/2020

Fallen

I find myself prostrate on the lawn
Mystified, muddled,
Staring blankly at the leaves and the blue
A big black and white dog licking my face.
Trying to remember, my mind brings up
My mom, dead these many years.
Perhaps I too have died
But surely the dead don't hurt THIS much.
The licking is the key, Beowulf's big tongue but
My head hurts.
My knee hurts
My back hurts and there is
A faint order of dog shit and damp grass

Fallen

We find ourselves prostrate on the streets
Mystified, muddled,
Staring blankly at black smoke and the blue
A snarling mongrel staring down at us.
Trying to remember our kindness, our humanity
Minds wandering aimlessly we try to focus.
But all we find is a distant past.
Memories of Mom and some long forgotten birthday party with
    balloons and friends
Riding in some old Buick all to watch the speedometer turn from
    99,999 to 100,000
And laughing together to celebrate, what?
Faint odors of smoke, dog shit, fireworks and damp grass

Fallen

We have fallen
Fallen for the hoax of political salvation
Fallen for the lies, for the BIG LIE.
Fallen

Risen

Tentative, fragile, we extend our hopeful selves
Helpless as newborn puppies weak as moonlight
We allow ourselves to hope for resurrection

11/21/2020

This Poem

Beowulf and I keep walking past this poem.
Carefully avoiding looking directly at it like
The butcher who can't see a fly in the meat cabinet.
There is a perfect duo of skinny spruce cones
Sitting on a palm shaped frond.
We pass it every day on the long walk
And think that this is the last time we will see them.
But every day, as if flaunting their independence
THERE THEY ARE
The two of them, challenging me to commit poetry
By not falling off the frond, even when encouraged to
By Beo's sweeping tail or a passing gust of wind.
There they sit as if glued
Challenging
Arrogant.
I refuse to write about them until they fall.

06/01/2020

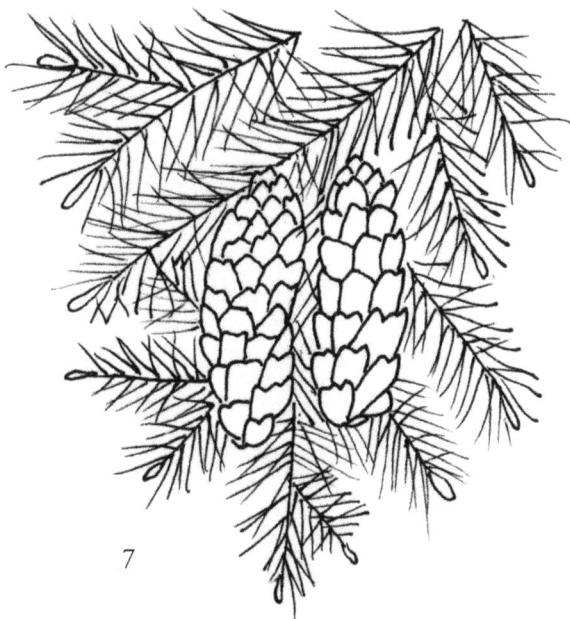

Boxing Day

On Boxing Day I gather them
Sadness, hate, love, disappointment, loneliness, apathy.
They hide beneath the sofa, among dust bunnies, behind the
    washer-dryer and in that curious drawer under the oven.
At the dog park they try to foil my efforts at control,
At the library they slither between bookshelves
At the gas station I catch them peeking from behind pumps.
Mercilessly, I box them up without wrapping, without ribbons,
    without tape, without styrofoam peanuts.
I put on gloves and pummel them with my best left hook, right
    cross combination until they lie on the canvas, panting with
    bloody exhaustion;
And yet they rise, undaunted, clinging to the ropes to fight again.

12/31/2018

Humans

We are
Savage
Combative
Warlike
Animals

We Kill
Each other
Other animals
To eat
For convenience

No One
Is free
Is safe from this
Sentence
From this life

We Are
Human
We kill
Each other
Over and over

06/25/2021

Beautiful Creatures

They flash silver from the sea and we eat them for snacks
They run through fields of grass and we eat them for dinner.
Pigs scream to live, and we make sausage for breakfast.
Gentle cattle are slaughtered for lunch with Beaujolais
And geese, feathered grace, feet nailed to the floor
Are force fed to fatten their livers
We kill and eat the beautiful creatures of our planet.
We kill them.
We eat them.
Those lesser occupants of the planet.
Like the fawn I passed on the highway today
Lying in the median, legs twisted in death
Its' lovely spotted hide smeared with mud and gravel.
And, yeah of course we kill each other
We kill each other but waste the meat.
We only kill each other for our need to kill
Cannibals had it right; but
We just kill each other to kill
Lust.

05/30/2021

Unleaving: for G.M.Hopkins

After the garage sale, broom in hand I see
A smudged and dirty phosphorescent ten cent price tag lying
   where the crippled cricket had struggled
Missing one of its' big back legs it struggled
Animated pentapod—across the wet and autumn driveway it
   struggled, dragging itself: to death.
Among the potted plants and fallen leaves the poor thing dragged
   itself.
Surrounded by the saleable and useless castoffs of my life.
Preparing for the sale I'd come upon momentos: baby books from
   both my kids, the chewed and broken corners speaking now to
   me of tiny loved and dripping baby mouths
My son, no longer child yet not adult just chuckled as he threw
   them in the trash.
The long forgotten things of children, wives and dead guys:
   Barbie's Beach House, and old paperbacks sat on tables near the
   rusty wood stove and the gleaming copper light salvaged from a
   dead and sunken ship.

Lurching tireless arthropod, my crippled cricket labored to where
   Peggy, pretty preteen girl in soccer clothes spied it
And stepping quicker than my shouted NO, she stepped on it
   with a tiny POP.
Her honey halo hair was brightly backlit as she scraped the tiny
   carcass from her soul.
Gazing down at the glowing tag among the wet and windblown
   leaves my heart, my guts turn over.
Exposing the soft and tender underbelly of loss of love, of life's chaos.
The sale of these sad things cannot absolve me from the things of
   man for which I care
I haven't got fresh thoughts about the swirl of old radios with
   broken knobs and houseplants and spectacles and vacuum
   cleaners, watches without hands or faces or even crystals
Time passes as do we, and yet
I cannot seem to scrape this sad and used detritus from my soul
   as I sweep tags and scraps of paper, rubber bands and Margaret's
   grieving leaves into a golden pile.

10/15/1995

The Bat

For Otis

A friend told me that I should get a cat
To ease my loneliness and kill the bat
Whose family lives up in my attic.
His cat had proven quite dramatic
Leaping up to get his flying mammal
As if shooting down a Sopwith Camel

The trouble is that I don't really need
Another mammal in my house, indeed
To kill a bat or mutilate a mouse
And fear aside, I certainly would grouse
That killing animals just isn't right
Although a cat is fighting nature's fight.

To eat this bat won't feed the cat a lot
And fit my vegan lifestyle it will not.

02/28/2021

A Citizen On His Brokeness

For John Milton

When I consider how my dough is gone
Ere all my years in this dark world an wide
And that small fortune which is death to hide
Lodged in some Harleys and a sodded lawn

And in Vermont some lovely mountain land
To serve therewith my family far flung
With a vacation spot to see the setting sun
But that question still remains at hand

Doth God exact day-labour cash denied
Is volunteering then at Meals on Wheels
Enough to fill my culture's deals
Or if I have no money do I simply hide?

The answer comes with fearsome haste
They also serve who only spend and waste

02/27/2021

For Otis Kidwell Burger

My sister called today to tell me you had died.
She'd heard from Anne that you died peacefully.
Well, not for me it isn't peaceful.
It's hellish sad and makes me angry.
Selfish anger 'cause I didn't get to New York in time.
I had my own and selfish occupations.
Machinery, grandkids, the Harley, the Jaguar, and
New York still was in the plan, but farther out.
You were farther out than I planned but
Your planning was superior to mine, 'cause
For certain there is a place where poets go
A joyous swelling of swirling words.
And you have joined Thomas, and Merwin, Stafford and
Coleridge and Donne, Stevens and Whitman and Kinnell
All of your words coming together in a symphony
That will speak to me always
You've joined all those poet's swirling, joyous rhymes
Of immortal anger, joy, fear and loathing
Pieces of humanity Pieces of us.
Fitting I suppose that you should die
In the month that celebrates poetry
Celebrates you, Otis.
I am sure that you
Did not go gentle

04/23/2021

15

Miracles for Ace and Diana

This baby unborn, absorbed my loving, agnostic, crippled prayers
    from a thousand miles toward the rising sun.
She is loved, parented and birthed by the wonders of modern life.
By you, parents free to choose from infinite paths.
We can kneel at the alter of Medicine/of Ego/of Today.
The future, yet unwritten, is for you and this baby to write after
    I am dust.
A frozen embryo carried in a thermos to be implanted by some doctor
From that womb of stainless steel into a warm and welcoming human
To become a human who will wade into the pool of us
To write the future
To write of a Science that can overcome these challenges yet
    cannot alter the feelings in our hearts.
Newborn, she holds our fragile feelings in her tiny hands.

08/29/2019

Searching

With the doggedness of Howard Carter
In the Valley of the Kings
I am searching
I turn over rocks of despair
I dig into sands of loneliness
I tunnel into ledges of dread
I crawl into caves of fear.
But Carter knew what he sought and I do not.
My confusion is tinged with hysteria soaked in wonder
And suddenly I spy the entrance
Yara Rose McArleton Gonzalez

04/23/2019

Picking Berries in Cemeteries in Vermont

The little one is stuffing her mouth as the dog lies quietly observing.
We watch
A bee, her pollen sacs loaded as she
Helps herself to more and more and more.
Stuffing her self with future honey
So we can watch her beezy work here and then she's
Home to waggle dance more of her beezy sisters here
And back here so the little one and I can watch
Her stuff her sacs
While the little one stuffs more of the cemetery's berries
And we go home to do the parent dance
As the dog lies quietly observing
Observing quietly
And we gather grapes off of loaded vines
In the yard of the old frame house on Hall Street
To make the dinner dance in the kitchen
Of the old frame house by the river in Winooski
Stuffed with love and berries

07/27/2020

Juneteenth

Today began like most national holidays
Rainy, warmish, but
This national holiday was declared only yesterday.
It celebrates emancipation.
Celebrates freedom.
Celebrates.
A day off from work
Now that's something to celebrate.
The damned cell phone vibrates on my nightstand
At this hour it has to be family calling.
With some kind of terrible news.
I struggle to sit
I struggle to find my specs
I struggle to find the right buttons on the phone
I struggle to find the buttons on my shirt
I struggle to clear my fuzzy head
And then I read
Elio Bay McArleton Gonzalez
Born 7:55am
8lbs, 5oz 21 inches
I collapse with delight, whooping
Now there's a national holiday for you.

06/19/2021

Mom's Kitchen

Suburban marsupial
She tucks a spoon into her pouch
As she glides more than walks
From stove to freezer to cabinet to sink.
I gaze in wonder from below the counter
At her fluid dance.
At her stirring and spooning and scraping as I wait
For the moment.
The moment
When I will share the bowl with my sister,
My co-conspirator.
We wait
To share
To lick the bowl from the cookie making marsupial
Who dances in the kitchen mixing eggs and sugar and
Tiny pieces of brown stuff from a yellow crinkly bag
With butter that she has let me hold to warm, to soften.
We are part of this quiet conspiracy of the apron pocket
Of the afternoon that waits for the arrival of the Buick
He will be happy to see us...
But he will never know the joy of bowl licking.
It is only for us three conspirators to know this secret joy.
He will only know the joy of cookies.

11/24/2020

Halley's Comet

For Frances Griffith Carleton

You told me of your wonder
When at the age of seven
Your mother took you out at night to see the comet.
You said the night was brighter than the full moon sky
And when it returned in 1985
I was in Tasmania and you were in Chicago
And the comet was a vast and smoky smudge
Across the Southern sky.

Last night as it yearly does
The Orianid Meteor Shower, remains of Halley's tail
Came to the skies over Michigan.
It showed me flashes of meteoric streaks
Some trailing smoke
All trailing memories of you and of Tasmania
Halley's comes again in 2060
Perhaps we will watch together

10/19/2020

For Jordan

On the night that we passed Munoz Human Cannonball on 23 it
   rained a bit.
His stake-bodied Chevy with cannon shaped like Breedlove's
   "Spirit" lurking huge, defiant, star spangled on the bed pulled
   an ancient Airstream.
Dented, aluminum, it woggled, washing back and forth behind
   the truck.
Just like the shiny lure I'm trolling with tonight, as sunset tells us
   of the coming darkness with phosphorescent pink.
Occasional fish rise up to look it over,
Flashing silver from deep inside the liquid Earth
Moving with a logic beyond and below us or Munoz,
We can feel the universe breathing
Waiting for us.

08/1995

Amaryllis I

This Christmas my dad came 'round.
Horticulturist and author, he certainly was here
Though dead these 20 years.
He was in the Amaryllis on the shelf
In front of the treadmill where I walk each day
Where I can concentrate on its' fragile and red and lovely
Blooms—the most I've seen
On any of these Christmas plants.
He's in this Amaryllis
And in this poem;
Although his poetry was born in the blood
Of World War One—a different splotch of red.
A different kind of hiding than he's doing now
In front of my treadmill and not the trenches.
He's peeking from behind the coffee maker,
From under the Himalayan salt lamp on my office desk
In the chips of this computer
Not in icy canvas tents on frozen European battlefields.
I miss his cranky ass and yet he's still around
In these clumsy lines
In this poem.

01/08/2021

Amaryllis II

This morning during my treadmill walking
I noticed with some surprise that
My Christmas Amaryllis
While the last of the fragile and
Red and lovely blooms was finally giving up and wilting
Had started to force another flowering spike
Up between the plump and verdant leaves.
Almost tentative, yet forceful it poked up toward light
The tip a greenish pinky hint of what's to come.
I am finding it hard to wait. I know he's coming.
Like a kid on Christmas Eve I wait
For the Old Man's return.
He's still hiding from me behind my keyboard
Behind this microphone
But sneaky, like that single sock missing in the drier
He's hiding there, a silent smile on his face
Surprise!
Daddy's home

01/25/2021

Hubert

I can see him now. Kneeling
The field of blooming daffodils engulfing him
To his waist.
A small almost delicate man
Once a raving Commie on a soap box at the depot
But now a flower grower not just of daffodils.
Tetraploid hemerocalis surge out of the fecund soil.
He bends forward, beckoning to them
Calling them out of the moist earth
Godlike in his beckoning
A small and delicate god
This flower grower, this beckoner
Dead these many years on Halloween
Indeed

05/09/2020

Meals on Wheels

We are driven.
We are driving carrots, breads, potatoes, onions
To the home bound, lonely, sick and sickly
The painfully human Humans in pain
We carry food to them in plastic bags and cardboard cartons.
To apartments, to houses
Wells of loneliness, homes of sadness.
They speak to us with kind or desperate voices
Or maybe not at all.
When we leave we carry more than we brought.
We carry
We drive
Today in the Super Blue Blood Moon
We are driving carrots, breads, potatoes, onions
And her teeth are falling out
And his dog is failing, dying
And he is moving to a rest home
And she has no legs
And she keeps all her plastic bags and envelopes
After route I fight my revulsion at the smell
And I am paralyzed with sadness
I have carried all the pain and sadness home
To me.
With me.

01/25/2018

Encephalitic Dream Quest

I read the other day of Tom
Who'd died at forty-one
Asleep since he was just thirteen.
His mother, sixty-four had bathed and cared for him
So well
That never had he had a rash or sore
In twenty-eight some years asleep.

But Tom, just think how strange it would have been
If you had leapt all cured from bed
And with your untold dreams of 1945
Stepped out to ride a monorail
Or strolled the city park at sunset.
How curious it would have been
To be a forty-one year old and captain of your junior high school
    football team,
Still a paper boy at heart.
Or stranger still would you have grown to full adulthood in the
    world of dreams?
Matured among the shades and misty shapes
To be the lord of Icthion or some enchanted country?

How worth it would have been for mom
To see you wake.

07/01/1970

Not the Sauce

Jill, your great mind has brought us to the edge of
Knowledge, the edge of the universe.
With your search.
Carl thought you were pretty cool.
But you managed to swerve around some big road blocks
On your journey.
Locked in your college dormitory from midnight to six
Pushed by counselors to do women's work
Like teaching first grade, or social work
You blew it all off and did science and engineering
Definitely not women's work.
You kept searching, looking up at the starry skies
Thinking that as you walked hand in hand with your dad
That somewhere out there in the galaxy
Another child was walking hand in hand with her dad.
Hand in hand with her dad on a beach not unlike
The beach in Florida where you walked on starry nights.
Somehow your six year old mind
Was preparing to reach out and search the cosmos
Search for that Extraterrestrial Intelligence.
Searching for her,
Searching for your cosmic doppelganger.

05/24/2021

Catherine Johnson

On the day you died at ninety-one and struggled years
A virus led the newscast
Followed by Harvey Weinstein's conviction
Followed by Coby Bryant's memorial.
Your death was an afterthought, a footnote, an also ran.
And yet
You were the real ground breaker
Real innovator
A woman innovator at NASA
A black woman innovator at NASA
Whose brilliant mind allowed Sheppard and Glenn
To escape the bonds of Earth and go to the Moon.
Innovator
Calculator
A hero
Not an athlete or a movie maker
Just a run of the mill mathematical genius
Who drove the girls to work in your old Chevy
A Catherine Johnson.

02/22/2020

Bodies

We shuffle in and out of pure and yellow light
Murmuring, looking, listening
Between Oriental and rubberized cadavers.
We look with mingled fear and fascination at bones and teeth and muscles.
And penises—so many rubberized and Oriental penises.
And yet it is not the penises or muscles or indeed the fear that hold us
But the chemical and cloying fog of preservation, of death.

Most of all however in our looking we fail to see
The bodies watching us.
We never catch them looking But they see:
Staring out through manufactured eyes
Set like gems in faces flayed of skin and flesh
Faces individual as ours even without skin, without flesh
We all have come to see and became the scene, unseen
Perhaps obscene.

10/24/2006

Tipping Point

I have hoarded, loved and mindlessly possessed things:
Art, Cars, Motorcycles
And alas, my 'cello.
The sound of the Bach 'Cello Suites live in my head
Ma, Rostropovich, Casals.
But tipped over, I must sell my beloved.
Glowing burgundy light burnished to perfection in
Germany in 1888, smooth curves front and back,
Between my knees I caressed her and she sang a duet
With my bow and hand, she sang
She sang of calm and lonely longing
Of love and loss and bright mornings
And now the tipping point.
My hand will never caress the finger board
Or move the bow in and out in just the right way.
My shaking hands rebel
Against her love and loss and bright mornings.
My hands have tipped me
To where I must release her to sing with another
May she sing for someone beautiful, beautifully.
Sing the hand duet with another and maybe, then
Maybe yet another now that I am past my tipping point.
I hope her songs will go on.

08/25/2021

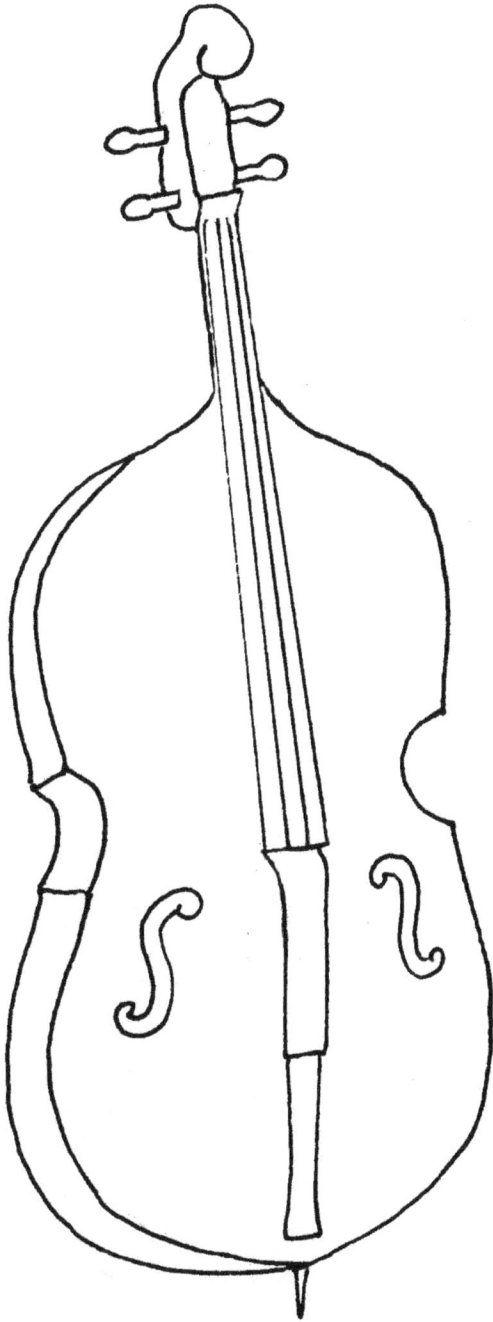

In Mexico

A crude hand lettered arrow points
Down the dusty weedy rutted street.
Six letters on a wooden arrow
A worn and dirty wooden arrow CORTES
In the humid Mexican morning
Looming jungle trees darken this weedy rutted street.
Dirty barefoot children play in noisy little groups
In front of the local church
Whose lovely stained glass Madonna peers out sadly
At the noisy little groups of dirty barefoot children.
Half a block deeper into the dark morning
Stands a crumbling homesite.
Unlike the one room huts that line the rutted street
This hacienda, once vast, outlined
By broken remains of walls, slaves quarters,
Of stables, bedrooms, a courtyard, a kitchen
The broken walls no more than a suggestion of a house.
In the living room a huge and ancient Banyan tree
Has overgrown the broken wall.
It looms over the ghost of a hacienda
Hanging roots seeking the soil that used to be
The floor of a tiled and formal dining room.

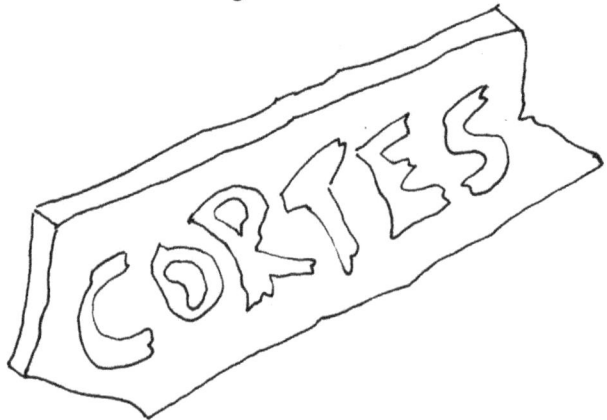

More dirty barefoot children climb and play
Among the rooms of roots and ruins
In this once formal dining room of
Conquistador Hernan Cortes
The murdering butcher of their ancestors.
Hundreds of years have tamed and flattened
His hacienda
His slave quarters
His head quarters.
Time has hidden a savagery
That civilization could not.

12/27/2020

Sir Francis

Mister Drake
Your equation, although limited
Tells me that the neighborhood is in all likelihood
Populated by other intelligent beings.
Other intelligent beings who
Blessed with big brains
Might not be blessed with emotions, like
Love
Empathy
Pity or simple
Kindness.
They might instead be hungry, or simply interested:
Looking down on us the way
My granddaughter watches ants on the sidewalk.
Her studied curiosity writ large on her small face
Without animosity or love.
Are these tiny crawling things tasty?
Will they play with me?
Perhaps the other will come for intergalactic plunder
Like water or granite or concrete.
Like Sir Francis, they may be circling the galaxy like
Privateers seeking loot for their queen
Or seeking queens as loot.

11/21/2020

Pripyat

A giant ferris wheel stands creaking slightly in the breeze
Deserted by the children, the cartoon character rides
Show three decades of decay of abandonment
This, a city of young marrieds is deserted now.
Now a city of dust and decay.
A city of dust and decay since April 26, 1986.
Atop a crumbling apartment block a sign
In large Cyrillic letters reads
"Let the atom be a worker not a soldier"
A railroad station
A post office
A grocery store
Still standing, windows broken, doors ajar
In the distance signs of massive construction
The world's largest Quonset hut
A railroad
Enough concrete for a sidewalk to the moon
Cranes, trains, Towmotors, workers in hard hats
All to cover reactor number four
To cover the sins of technology carelessly used

But in the thick woods around the now deserted site
Life continues to struggle with our carelessness.
Life doesn't need a railroad
Or a grocery store
Or a Towmotor
Or cranes
Life doesn't thrive for concrete
But in the green and verdant forest
Animals are stirring, growing, breeding
Perhaps an extra head on a snake
Or a fifth leg growing out of a rat's belly
Or the feral deer with an extra antler.

Life continues to struggle with man nonetheless
The site abandoned.
The atom was indeed the worker.

04/26/2021

For Lee

We are stumbling now through an undiscovered country.
A county that you and I are passing into
I want to explore it
Examine it
Live it
Discover it with you.
But sadly it resists discovery
It encourages exploration while discouraging answers
It challenges life
This country is shrouded in a fog so dense that It defies all vision
And yet we peer at it with eager need.
We peer at it with hunger for the answer
And yet we know it is unknowable, shrouded.
Only the young are oblivious to its' magnetism
They just about rear end us
As we, gaping open mouthed
In the middle of this road
Have halted to peer into the dense and challenging fog
Peer into age
Peer into empty wisdom

06/13/2021

For Bob

Lee called me this morning and told me
The awful news that you had died
You didn't pass away You died
Without warning you just died.
I sit before this page, this poem of remembrance
Remembering how you talked to my dad,
Taking horticulture as your calling, and
I remember that Triumph Tiger 100 and the cop
That stopped me and took so many photos
And how you asked me to pick up that antique Evinrude.
On my way home from Vermont.
I remember when we bought that '55 Eldorado,
Those dual quads under the golden triangle air filter
It was so rusty the doors wouldn't even latch.
And the '49 Buick Sedanette, and the antique hearse
That cherry '52 Hudson Wasp for which
We paid the princely sum of fifteen dollars.
You stoked my love of mechanical devices
And here I am in the gear business.
Sadly, Hudson Motor Car Company is gone from
Ypsilanti and all the other cars and bikes and junk
Have died a slow and rusty death fading to gone.
I miss them all.
I miss you, Bob

03/16/2021

Remaking Earth

We build things.
I pass borrow pits at every overpass
On this concrete and Midwestern trail
At Luckey Haskins and Wapaconeta where
Neil's concrete skull cap of a museum
Swells up from farmland beside the trail
At Bluelick where building after giant steel building
Scatter around the farms
And towers, so damned many steel towers
Rise up, so many steel mantises
Ready to snatch a passing school bus full of girl scouts.
Power lines vanish into the summer haze
And United States Plastics tells me
In large friendly letters that "Christ is the Answer"
And I mutter in passing; "But what is the question?"
Three giant rain drops splatter on the windshield dust.
I drive into the darkening sky of evening.

09/20/2020

Broken

My poems have suffered
From this broken shoulder
One finger typed with terrible slowness
Terrible thoughtfulness
Terrible deliberation
The self pity is clinging like honey,
Like napalm to a dying Vietnamese child.
Until my restless mind stumbles onto Hawking
Onto shame
Onto inspiration

03/20/2019

Intruder

Sitting at the desk hammering on my keyboard
I was startled by a sudden movement:
Just a bat circling the office. A BAT?
Circling The office.
I was terrified
By this sudden movement
By this sudden intrusion.
This tiny flying mammal
A tiny flying mammal in the office
On a freezing and February day.
What to do?
Stymied, I put on an old fedora:
To what?
Give the little guy a place to settle down to raise a family
Or to keep the guano out of my fast receding hair?
After many months, I am still unnerved by this intruder.
In this old house: this century old house.
This century old house has been the bat family's home
For all these years.

Who, indeed is the intruder?

02/21/2020

A Man of Hats

I have become a man of hats.
My house is festooned
With fedoras, packed
With Panamas and capped
With Kangols, not to mention bulging
With ball caps and boaters.
I can accept being an old man
I come by it honestly.
But my father is here as well.
This time he's no potted plant
He's in the old top hat that sits on the shelf;
The old top hat that he wore to the opera
With the tuxedo, the silk scarf, white gloves and spats.
He lingers in that old hat,
And in this poem.

10/21/2021

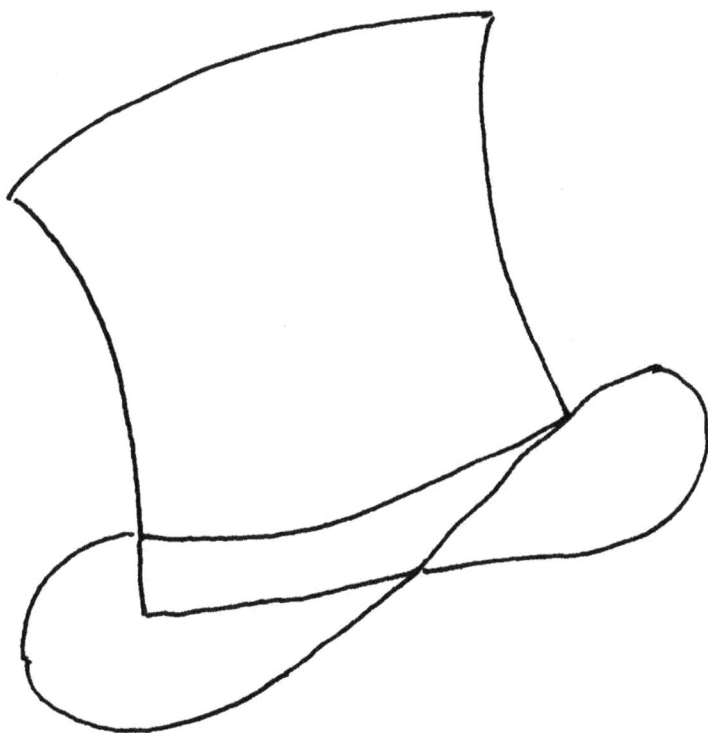

Northern Lights

When I was ten, at our vacation home in Maine
Mom and Dad woke me in the middle of the night
To show me Aurora Borealis, those
Waving curtains of purple and green.
They scared me shitless.
I stood silently terrified, trembling from cold and fear.
Trembling from life
Trembling from the awful knowledge that I was
Witnessing the end of the world.
Back in my bed I trembled
Ashamed.
I never told them
Ashamed
I wanted to tell them.
I wanted to tell the scary curtains to go away,
To tell Mom and Dad to keep me safe.
Even now I want to confess my terrors
Death,
Nuclear war
Cancer and the like.
Ashamed

02/16/2020

Melville Keeps Following Me

Herman, your epic has followed me, cetology and all
From central Illinois to Maine
From Maine to Illinois again
And on to Michigan.
In cartons, plastic totes and bags.
Next to the OED
On shelves of boards and piles in corners.
You never gave up Herman
You never faltered.
Just a bit of mildew on the corner of the cover
The odd highlight on a line or two here or there
And yet you never did convince me to finish your epic.
I really wanted to.
I was taught that it was the foundation of America Lit,
And yet I couldn't do it.
Couldn't quite focus well enough
Couldn't hold your brilliance well enough
Couldn't stay with it...
But maybe someday I can
Reach up to the shelf next to the OED...

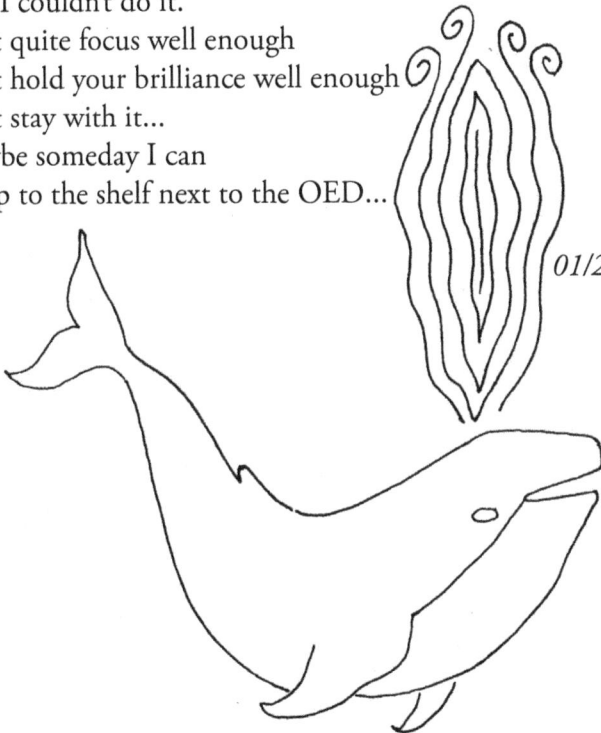

01/20/2020

Love Poem

On this brown and February afternoon
I dream of spooning you,
While ice coats trees and power lines and buildings
As the wheels come off of love and
I commence to leak love and need and knowing you.
I shall never spoon you again while
Ice comes down covering my heart like falling snow.
Ice is squeezing my heart like potter's hands
Your hands, your sex so gently squeezing
Until at last the last tree branch snaps
Power lines sag down until they snap and lie there
Waiting for the innocent to touch their deadly sting
My heart becomes as still as buildings, as cold winter,
As sad as country music.
Please, oh please just help me hate you.
Help the rage and angst boil inside of me
So that hating you allows me to go on.
I need the rage to start my iced up heart again.
Somewhere in these powerless and broken lines
I need to learn to hate the way I loved you.

02/13/2017

Enola Gay

There were four of us
Playing poker at Clayton's kitchen table
In his Maine and white and island home
Hard men
Fisher men
Lobster men
Drinking, cursing, winning, losing.
Taking a break I walked into the parlor and
Looking at the bookshelves I saw
A fragile Japanese and tiny tea cup decorated
With delicate figures on a mountain path.
A path that ended at a lump of melted glass
Clinging to the translucent rim.
When Clayton came into the room I passed him the cup
And asked about it. He passed it back.
It felt warm in my calloused hand.
He told me that he
Was with the first troops to enter Hiroshima
After Little Boy fell from the Enola Gay in 1945.
He found the little cup in the rubble.
We stood there in his parlor fifty years ago, yet
Still my palm can feel the warmth, the heat, the shame.
My old friend Clayton is long gone now
And I am no longer a lobsterman
But my palm has never lost the sad, the terrible warmth.

02/07/2018

Tim

We were in a college dorm room
A dorm room that smelled of socks and smoke,
Smelled of teenage sweat and socks and smoke.
Five kids, playing poker, faking sophistication
Carefully not noticing anything odd
Casually pretending to be casual,
Normal teenage kids
Cursing, drinking tepid beer
Drinking and cursing.
Drinking cursing and smoking.
Just kids
Ante up
Pot right?
Baseball
Five card stud
Four kids holding cards in smoke-yellowed fingers
Tim, the smartest held the cards with his flippers
We pretended not to notice.
Drinking, smoking, cursing
Casually not noticing Thalidomide Boy

12/25/2020

If I Walked

I have seen you thirty or more times on these cold and rainy and
   Polish streets,
Your tall and sexy form just slipping around corners or
Ducking into doorways in these stone and ancient buildings
But you always seem to evade me, climbing into taxis,
Zooming off
Before I can touch or even speak to you.
Careening off on a bicycle or roller blades, even stepping into
   trains as they pull away.
All of Eastern Europe mocks me:
Pretending to be you.
I cannot reach you in life or dreams.
I cannot touch or taste you as I lie here in this hotel bed.
Frustrated, dreaming of walking in the autumn woods
Where leaf mold lies like Margaret's golden grove unleaving.
And I am dreaming like Margaret:
Dreaming of a time before your youth and beauty made me run
   from you.
If I walked in heaven I would walk with you.

09/04/2004

Rats With Wings

A lovely grey of wing with black tips
A blindingly white head with intense red eyes
A sunny yellow beak with paler feet
Wheeling overhead as I dump expired bait
Into the flat grey Atlantic
They dive for the rotting treats
With screams like children playing in a pool
A banquet
A prize worth fighting for
A song of food.
These lovely Herring Gulls are hated
By the Maineiacs
These very Herring Gulls are filled with graceful beauty.
Even
A certain nobility
As they wheel in the wind.

It thrills me now when I see them here in Michigan
On lakes or ponds or garbage dumps.
I am a Maineiac lost in the Middle West.
A lobsterman without a boat
A writer without a cause
Except for the humble seagull.

04/04/2021

Time Pieces

I have collected them
These pieces of time
Over the years they have reached out to me
A hundred or more times.
My grandfather's hunting case Elgin
A gift from the Apollo Club of Duluth in April of 1904
His lovely tenor voice reaches across the years,
A century and more.
And the elegant Doxa Anti Magnetique
From the same year,
Its' silver case shows
A horseman in top hat and tails jumping a fence
At some forgotten dressage event.
An American Waltham is unadorned and clean
Its' Roman numerals slim and delicate
Its' hands reach out to me
From some old railroad worker's railroad days
I have collected time many times.
More than a hundred years' worth
A piece of him
A piece of all of us
A piece of time

02/14/2021

Surviving

I am surviving at Home
Remote as a Bhutanese monastery
Surviving here
I feel the virus closing in
On
Me.
I feel the aloneness closing in
On
Me, surviving.
I feel my sanctuary closing in
On
Me, surviving here.
The Lizard waits
For
Me
Huge head hovering like a statue on distant Rapa Nui
Observable as quarks
The Lizard waits
It
Waits silent.
Coyote
Waits

03/13/2020

Sequoia

I stand
The tallest
The most board feet of any sentinel
But even I am threatened.
A forest of my fellows gathers in NoCal

Us

Those sentinels are where we spread Hubert's ashes.
They are threatened.
Are burning,
Even though protected by our laws
Threatened by us
Even though protected by nature
They are burning.
These giants shrug off a mere forest fire
But they can't survive mankind's stupidity
Mankind's ignorance
Man's shrugs

Firefighter

We cannot win.
Defeated by the drought
Defeated by the climate change
Defeated by ignorance
Defeated by shrugs

09/19/2021

Wars

Our language has deteriorated.
But then again, it goes along with the deterioration
Of US.
Of USA
Of USUAL
Face it. We're savages
Animals.
But lions don't mind killing to feed the cubs
Wolverines parents need to return to the cave with food
Killer Whales will kill migrating Blue Whale calves
Despite the mother's
Suffering to save her calf.
And we, of course eat other mammals
But TV tells us of Star Wars
Cake Wars
Animal Fight Night
Holiday Wars.
Storage Wars
We are Desensitized

11/06/2020

Saigon Again

When we lost the war in Viet Nam
My friends and I celebrated when
The helicopters lifted off from the roof tops
Desperate Vietnamese children clinging to the skids.
Planeloads of collaborators struggling to get airborne
Told the story of our victory over a government
That conscripted and controlled our friends
And made enemies of the anonymous Asians.
We had temporarily won our war against war
Sure, the draft was replaced by "volunteer" soldiers
And we now have a Space Force
But losing a war was new to our bloody government
Losing was just temporary
Until I saw the helicopters fleeing Kabul this morning
The difference?
Neither war was ever winnable.
But the resistance to this war was weak,
Perhaps the weakness of youth
Perhaps the weakness of youth defeated by internet
Perhaps the strength of religious fanaticism.
Clearly, we all have lost the war on war.
Permanently
Now on to the Climate Change, lots more to lose there
If only anyone would care.

08/15/2021

Ladder

There is a ladder on my back porch.
A step ladder, an aluminum step ladder
The ladder leans against the wall next to the door
It has leaned there for months: waiting.
At last: this summer, something
A bird.
This bird, a robin, moved in while I was traveling.
Moved right in, building her nest on that top step
Where I always put my tools, paint brushes or nails
The step with the warning not to step there.
The bird obeyed the sign, not stepping, just building.
She was a sloppy builder, twigs and grass all over.
My porch looks like a badly kept horse stall
This bird is not happy with my comings and goings
She dive bombs me whenever I approach the door
Or even park in the driveway.
I have given up using the back door.
Robin 'o' Locksley or even Batman and Robin
Couldn't have done better at driving me off.
I've tried to tell her that I have no hostile intent.
No use.
I just hope her plot and her eggs are soon hatched.
I am embarrassed by my squeamishness
A bird, indeed.
My house, indeed

07/06/2021

They Also Serve

The stone ledge forces cold into the bones of my ass
As I sit here in Prague reading science fiction outside of the
    Cathedral of Saint Vidas.
The military color guard keeps marching past
The Cadence kept by shrill voiced callers.
They march past the stained glass windows and the gold and silver
    angels, gold and silver forest creatures.
Eagles and falcons holding forest mammals in their gold and
    silver talons.
Chubby little gold and silver Cupids with bows and quivers full
    of little arrows.
I am waiting.
Waiting for my friends
Waiting to drink a Pilsner Urquel, ambrosia of Prague
Watching the afternoon pass
Watching the color guard pass again.
Watching

05/09/2019

Sir David

Of late I am surprised to find myself in tears in front of some or
  other damned TV show.
A cop kneeling on someone's neck or
Maybe David Attenborough speaking in his lovely cultured British tones.
Relating how a starving polar bear or an orca needs to find a meal or die.
But the "meal" has to get away or die; so
I watch with the fascination of a rubbernecking driver creeping by
  a fatal highway crash
Or a bystander in Minneapolis
As some small and young and helpless fawn or whale calf is slaughtered
  so a more powerful animal can live or maybe feed its' young.
Or some bull walrus lords it over twenty females on the beach in
  the Arctic cold, and kills weaker rivals that show up to try and
  find a mate.
Power
Curious this world

04/24/2020

Rehearsal: White Chairs

At James Madison Academy in Las Vegas
There was a dress rehearsal for the graduation
The Second Amendment to the Constitution
Was addressed by two NRA luminaries
Who spoke of the need for gun rights
To maintain freedom and equality for the people
They were to address the attendees about 1776,
The flag, that well regulated militia
And how we, the people need to keep and bear arms
For home defense, self defense.
And how the first move that the Nazis made
Was to impound all the guns in private hands.
Guns don't kill, people kill.
It was a brief rehearsal.
The sound people setting the microphone levels
The speeches booming out on the empty field of
White chairs,
Three thousand white chairs.

Happily there was no graduation. There is no academy
It was all a false front to embarrass the NRA.
Sadly, it didn't work.
They cannot be embarrassed.
They are embarrassing

06/24/2021

Sternman

I lean over the gunwhale
Straining to see
In the blue green black and swirling sea
The potwarp sings a song of strain
Snapping a rhythm
Of work
Of fog
Of the rising sun burning a road of light across the slate grey
    surface from No Mans Land to our old and smelly boat
Of herring gulls wheeling overhead.
Looking down the potwarp I see
A swirling flash of movement as the trap spins up to me.
Full of lobsters, wrinkles, sea cucumbers, crabs, codfish and sea urchins.
Full of food
Full of lives—I have snuffed out so many lives.
I am the Ancient Mariner with out a crossbow; but
Guilty
A stern man
A sternman
The Paul Tibbets of the high seas.

03/23/2018

Escape

This train keeps passing through dark forests
And I see ravens from this old and Polish train.
Dark as Coca Cola they glide down to earth
And when they land I can almost hear them speak.
In voices raspy:
Voices old as this strange medieval country
That passes by the train window like a ruined movie set.

Fog settled on the factory three days ago and forced me
To trade an airplane for this shabby and Polish train.
Fog softens the passing country
And makes the forests seem blighted, enchanted.
The spare white tree trunks rise strange in the muted light of noon.
Their branches stretch spiderweb fine against a grey and ruined
    castle on a hill above the tracks.
And we speed up, slow down, speed up, slow down
Passing through each small and Polish town
To continue on to Berlin, to Frankfurt.
This train keeps passing through dark forests and depressing foggy towns.
Yet nothing can depress me I am coming home to you.

03/15/2007

Wheelhouse

In 1957 I was in awe of the Mary A
As she sat at a sagging wharf in Rockland, Maine.
Eighty feet of sagging trawler
Converted to the Matinicus mailboat.
Captain Stuart Ames, diminutive, handsome
Scrambled monkeylike to load the freight.
He accepted our fares and we stumbled aft
To the cramped and smelly passenger cabin
Our tickets torn from a roll like at a carnival ride.
Matinicus residents rode in the wheelhouse.
Away from the straphangers from New York
Away from us they rode in the wheelhouse.
Worse yet, we were from Chicago, home of Al Capone,
Even Mayor Daley
The Maineiacs didn't mix with summer complaints.
But I was a kid and somehow kids were immune.
Even Chicago kids were OK.
Thirty years later I moved to the island after college
To work as a lobsterman.
Captain Norris just crooked his finger at me
When I climbed aboard the Mary A to go to the island
And pointed to a seat in the wheelhouse.
With the most casual of nods, heart hammering
I took my place in the wheelhouse.
With a Masters degree from a Big Ten University,
My big thrill was riding in the smelly old wheelhouse.
I wonder if I return in 2022 will the captain
Crook a finger at me and point to a seat in the
Wheelhouse.

03/26/2021

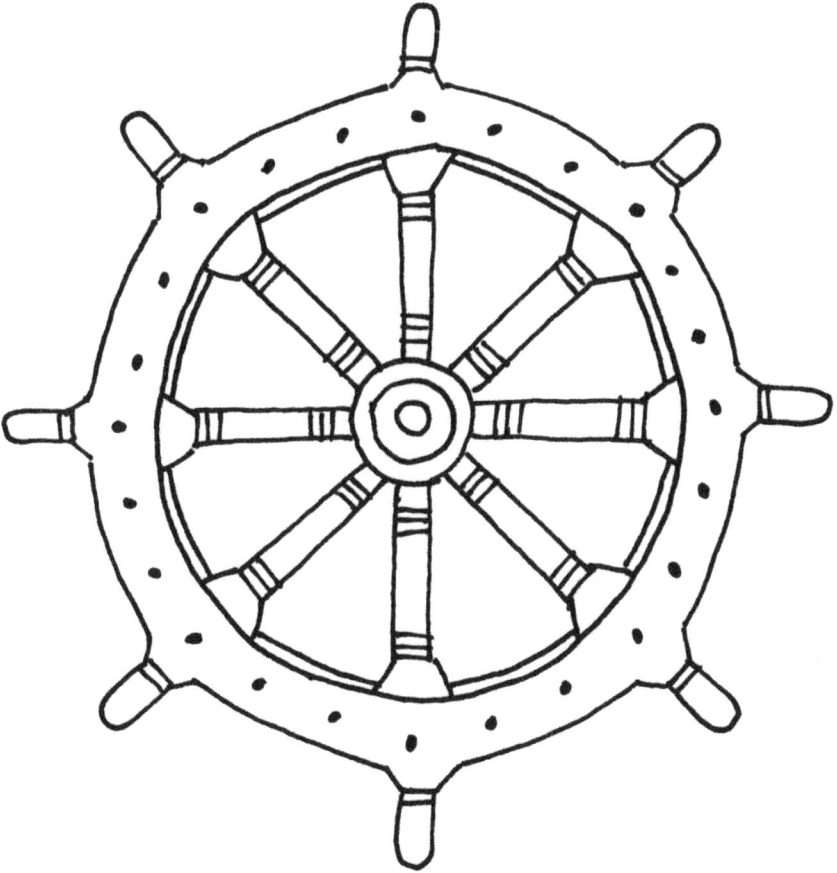

Recycle, Ode to a Tiny Lobster

Now you are just perfect
Hollowed out by hungry ants then
Dried by the sun
Your beautiful green and red colors preserved by shellac.
Bilateral symmetry preserved, two claws,
Eight fragile legs and a tail with flippers intact
Even antennae
Poised on the bookshelf, you could almost be alive
And yet, I killed you.
Casually, without a thought to your complexity
I killed you.
My wife understood how calloused I had become
Lobster fisherman,
Tough guy mariner
She tearfully hated even having you in the house.
I should have seen what she saw
I should have known I would regret the harm
That I did to your world
To our world
Please accept my apology, my prayer,
My cowardly plea for forgiveness
I finally learned from you that
We shall all be recycled
We shall be just perfect.

09/04/2021

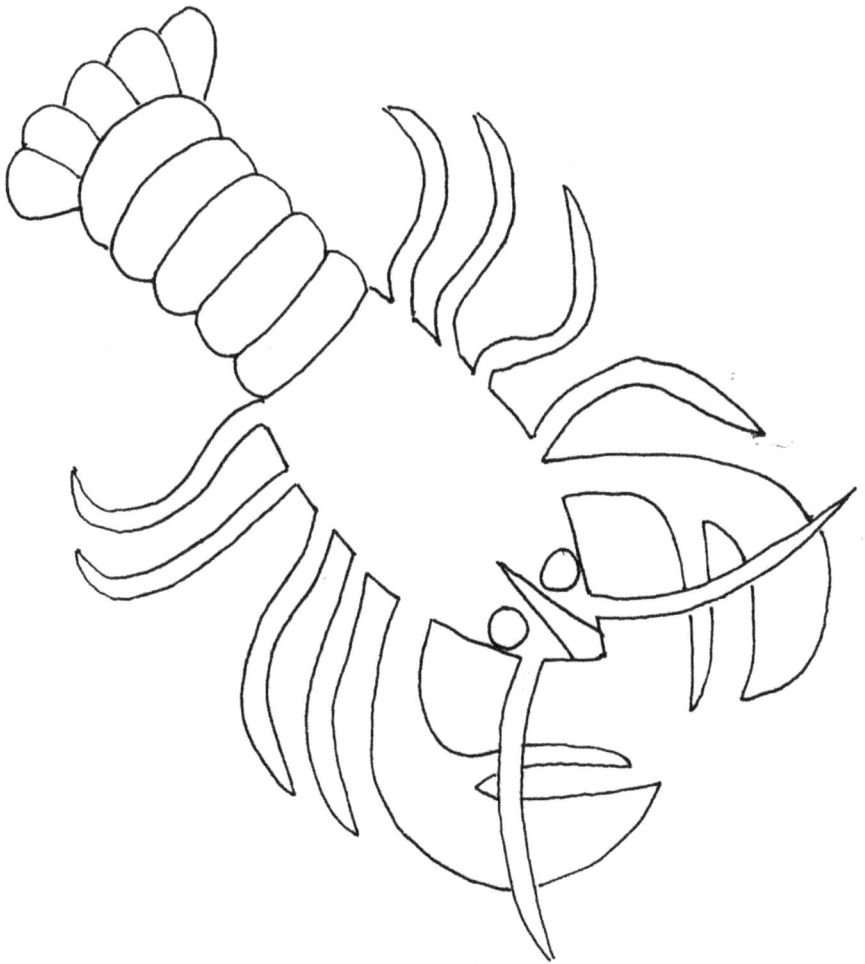

Ode to Tiny Green Snake

You hide from us, Sibling Searchers in the orchard
Under old tarpaulins, weathered boards, small flat stones and
   discarded cartons.
Cooled by the green mowed grass.
Shaded by acres of apple trees flowering in the warm Spring sun.
Warm away from early Spring frost and the cooling fog that steals
   in on Southeast breezes.
Green and supple you wind timidly around and between our fingers
Like glorious green and supple living jewelry.
Tiny ruby eyes in your tiny head investigating our mom
Who screams at your green snakeness,
At your ruby eyes, as you decorate our hands,
Living jewelry.
Always trying to find escape from our hands
Trying to return to the cool beneath the apple trees.
To the safety of greenness
The safety of the grass
The safety of the fog
Of the orchard in the Matinicus Spring

03/14/2021

Moving Experience

Again I am moving house.
Arduous, long and lonely work with which,
Although many have asked I cannot be helped.
It is the tiny discoveries that prevent help.
It is the tiny discoveries that keep me joyful,
Keep me mystified
Keep me working.
A small and wrinkled photograph of my daughter's birth
A beautiful shillelagh with a morel on the fist end
Spices that I have forgotten how to use
Hide behind the prunes
Spices that I have forgotten that I owned
Grow old along with me in the dusty cabinet.
Foreign coins from places I have forgotten
Join lint balls in sagging jacket pockets.
Old love letters from forgotten lovers
Wrinkled photographs of forgotten lovers
All conspire to make me doubt my sanity.
All these lonely works and tiny discoveries
Lurk behind other lonely works and tiny discoveries
And create a hidden me
Another me

10/25/2020

Spawning

Struggling upstream, exhausted, scarred, returning
To the pools where they were hatched.
Harassed by bears and eagles
Challenged by rapids and waterfalls
They are determined to find those pools
To lay their precious eggs or have them fertilized
To create their masterpieces, their natural art.

Struggling out of bed at dawn, I stumble to return
To the chair that I left last night.
Harassed by emails and robocalls
Challenged by writer's block and text messages
I am determined to find inspiration
To lay down the perfect precious words
To create a poetic masterpiece
Hoping to finally reach my natural art.

Yet, block looms over me like a Rappa Nui statue
Staring toward a distant goal, a distant poem.
Remote as Madagascar and Mysterious as Bhutan
My natural art retreats, just beyond my feeble grasp.
Unfertilized.

07/12/2021

Church Tower

Today I had no work, and noticed how I missed you.
As if by chance I had mislaid my arms or legs or teeth
Or maybe my mind, faithless trickster, and yet
I cannot lose it, even if I wish.
It feels your absence over these kilometers,
These oceans, these forests.
And yet the trickster
Keeps on thinking all the time.
Why is it that I cannot turn it off?
Uncontrollable as atoms it keeps on thinking.
Wandering back to you.
Undisciplined and without the slightest care for me
The damned trickster bangs on about confusion and loss
So I climb this tower in this old and cold and Polish town
Surely this is some Freudian joke about climbing stairs
A three hundred step joke about stairs and you.
These three hundred steps should vanquish the trickster.
Alas, the three hundred fail.
The trickster creeps out again
On the twisting spiral descent.
Keeps insisting that I love you.

03/27/2007

The Mountains of Greenland

Today, after two and exhausting days of travel
I see them down below me.
White as refrigerators
Erupting from the flat and Greenland landscape,
Impassive as time, they lie there;
With glaciers calving icebergs into the ocean
Square and alabaster boats the icebergs float
Spreading out, frozen alabaster boats,
Organized as soup
Cold as Lapland
Lonely as the last two weeks of teaching engineering
To Polish engineers through interpreters and gestures
And now I am flying over Goose Bay, Gander, Montreal
And soon the flying stops
The waiting stops

03/29/2007

The Coriolis Effect

The Missouri cornfields are brown and whisper in the breeze.
The soybeans turning yellow by the wide Missouri mutter soft replies.
And we're passing through Tightwad, Missouri on Joplin's
    Memorial Highway.
We've been to Kansas, Missouri, Illinois, Indiana
So my friends can pedal on the Katy Trail.
Fifty miles a day through tiny towns abandoned by the rails
Tiny towns left behind in acrid dust like deserted lovers waiting
    sadly by the phone.
Booneville, Augusta, Marthasville, and Dutzow.
In tiny Portland Holzhauer's Bar and Grill beckons
With Fat Tire's open arms,
And I sit with local cowhands in the dark and funky tavern until
    time to pick them up.
We keep passing limestone cliffs, miles and miles of limestone
    cliffs above the sluggish river
Flowing past the limestone cliffs to meet the Gateway Arch, the
    beginning of the West, the end of our trip
A final lunch at the ancient train station in St Louis
And we are gone.
And looking back we see the widening gyres, ascending sacred
    lights above the Gateway.

06/28/2018

Steel of West Virginia

The three of us are walking
Walking through the dark and noisy plant
Walking in muck and greasy, searing heat
Lurching, Frankenstinian, stiff legged.
Occasional tongues of flame lick from unknown openings.
With a loud clank and crash.
An orange circle of steel crowns in the opening of an ancient
   rusted die set,
Blasting us with a wave of heat,
Only to be pulled back from the crowning
To emerge again
To be pushed fully into the world as
Newly formed channel steel.
We gaze in wonder at this ancient beginning
But we continue through the dark and moist and slippery tunnel
   toward the sunlight of the loading dock.
Emerging into brilliant light we draw first gasping breath

09/20/2018

Paris

That night when we ate at Le Procope
We were tourists from toes to eyeballs.
We ate overpriced roasted potatoes and roasted chicken
Even haricots vert.
I stood, and nonchalant I headed to the toilet,
Only stopping to sit down at Voltaire's writing table.
The brown marble was cracked and dirty; but
To me it was the best of all possible desks.
Memories are from the best of all possible lives.
This meal with Mom and Shelley and Nancy
This meal meant more
Meant more

01/11/2018

For Chloe

Chubby little puppies
Week old black and wrinkled hungry babies
Suck mama's milk
And sleep
Not even guessing The coming surprise Eyes

11/11/1976

Shayna

Sweet little beagle
You were rescued
From a cage.
A twenty-four inch box
That you existed in so you could ensure the safety of some cosmetic.
And my friend rescued you
Gave her loving self to you, loving gentle dog
You loved my friend as she loved you.
Happy playing in the yard pup
Rescued from a box
Rescued from that tiny prison
To her forever home.

11/17/2019

Shayna Dreaming

She sees the squirrels
She hears the crickets and
She smells moist earth as
She dog dreams of bounding through this forest
Whimpering
Legs jerking
In the dreaming world of dappled morning light and raven croaks
    and earthen smells she is young again;
But when she wakes, arthritic legs move stiffly,
And she is baffled by her blindness and deafness.
But there is beauty still.
Her nose can see the cool and moist and autumn world.

06/09/2018

Shayna Dying

The wind blew lovely pastel Autumn leaves down wet and shiny
   Cross Street
As Shayna, emaciated by the cancer walked demented, deaf blind
   circles in the wet and cold and lonely Autumn grass.
Randi held her gently all the way to the office
Held her in a gentle loving embrace
Silent tears, shaky hands
A lonely Autumn embrace
All the way to the office of the killer.
God, she loved that dog.
The vet came into the "caring room"
And Randi held her as the needle went in.
All three of us cried silent tears of regretful love
As we killed that sweet little dog.

11/12/2019

Ode to Lucia

Name like a Saint
Face of a comedian
Heart of a champion
Soul of an angel

You were brachiocephalic
And impossibly patient
With a herringbone pattern
On your back and funny ears

You walked with my Beo and your family
On the street in front of my old house
Savoring the olfactory buffet
The canine drug of choice

We will all miss you
Miss your quirky presence
Miss your loyal love
Miss your dogness

09/03/2021

A few words about the haiku

I admire the haiku as a form of poetry. It forces the poet to think clearly about one thing. I freely admit that I often don't follow the rules. I have never read the great poets who wrote haiku in ancient Japan: Basho, Issa, Katsuri, etc; but I have read them in translation, and I think I know the rules well enough to violate them. I violate them regularly, as I am wont to do with all the rules that face me in life. Generally we regard the haiku as a poem of seventeen syllables in three lines, with five syllables in the first line, seven in the middle line and five in the third line. Those who write "haiku" in English, like the fabulous Richard Wright adhere to this form, to which I also try and stick; but I violate the rule that the haiku is its' own title. I sometimes feel the need to use a title—so sue me. Call me a loner, a rebel, a bad poet... Several of my favorites follow.

Haiku number 102

I don't think I will
Ever be laid to rest,
I Am simply restless

Haiku number 19

As a myopic
Child eyeglasses changed the stars
From blobs to pinpoints

Haiku number 35

This morning news brought
Tears, horses crying, dying
In western wildfires

Haiku number 30

If you want to know
How to win don't study the
Wins, just the losses

Haiku number 31

On the way to work
A road killed fawn on a cool
Frosty Spring morning

Haiku number 202

Shakespeare, a poet
And a falconer left us
Many common terms.

Haiku number 61
"The N Word"

This violates the rules in at least two ways: a title, and an explanation of the thoughts; but what the hell is poetry for if not to violate rules? It was inspired by the use of the term "N Word" by one of my favorite writers, the Polish Sci-Fi master Stanislav Lem. He wrote a story which used the element Sodium as the N word; or Na which is the symbol for Sodium on the Periodic Table of the Elements.

No, negative, not
Normal, nowhere, Sodium
These are my N words

Haiku number 40
"Buddha is in the excrement scraping stick"

Walking in Milan
I imagine Budda
In the selfie stick

Haiku number 34

On my arms in front
Of me I see my father's
Hands—bony, spotted

Haiku number 101

Panthers, butterflies
Snarl, buzz and flutter past me
Lonely memories

Haiku number 50

I do admire the
Butter sculptor's labors
Ephemeral art

Haiku number 29

A faded old barn
Says "Chew Mail Pouch Tobacco"
Turns slowly to dirt

My Father

Born at the last gasp of the 19th Century, my dad volunteered for the Army and fought in WWI. He hated the trenches and the mud and the mules that he had to lead as a member of the Quartermaster Corps. And he wrote a lot of that down in some bloody brutal poems. I won't put any of that in this book.

He wrote books about plants and gardens. Pretty tame stuff. But in secret he wrote some poems, and I will put a few of those in here; perhaps so my readers could understand me a little better.

Enjoy!

10/27/2021

*News item: "The bishops further agreed that
the spiritual welfare of the troops demand that
chaplains be provided to every company"*

You fatted fools!
Decked out in silk and lace,
Slobbering in your padded stalls
Like blooded cattle bred for show
Pretending service to the One
Who hung in shameful death between two thieves
Because he scorned the puny jealousies
And hatreds of his day.
Who preached instead of love--
How can you sit complaisant and aloof,
Sipping tea, and gossiping
Of trivial, inconsequential things,
While men crawl like vermin on the ground,
While they writhe in agony
And lie beneath the bitter moon
As overhead the hurtling steel
Keeps off those who might relieve
Their frightful agony and pain?
Why do you not rise accusingly
And thunder at the presidents and kings
Whose hurt and silly pride
Must be appeased with blood?
Is it because you are afraid?
Afraid to be different from the herd?
Afraid to be called pacifist
In tones that plainly say
That snakes and pacifists are one?
Or do you really think
America and God now wage
A common war?

Go back then, you doddering fools
Rot in your oafish calm
And let us die
Without the pale!

R. Milton Carleton
12/1917

Release

And now the aching beat
Of mind against the throb of thought,
The troubled, bruising feet
Of imaged ghosts that stalk
Through memory's tortuous street
Are stilled.

No more is terror dark in flight
Against the bitter winter's moon;
Black wings soughing through the night
Sigh out to nothingness,
While I, released from fright,
Find peace in you.

R. Milton Carleton
Undated

Creation

Dust of shattered stars,
Brooding dark in Cosmos,
Fulfilling destiny,
Burst time's womb,
Filling the yearning night
Of aching space
With unbounded, limitless fire.

Swift, swift, swiftly speeding
Through Chaos,
Down Eternity,
At last in bounded orbit
Tied by force
To the centering sun,
Earth is born.

Fiercely raging flames,
Consuming their own passion,
Waver and die;
Cooling rocks, laved by rising seas,
Lie naked in the searing sun.

Primordial slime and nascent green
Cloak the naked stone;
Welling into emeraude tides
To flow across the budding earth.

R. Milton Carleton
Undated

Expectancy

Dearest, beloved,
Part of me;
These waiting months are nearly gone:
Soon from out your frame
Life will tear new life.

Fear holds me when I think of your pain,
The agony of your cross
Which purposes that from yourself
May spring a new stream
To swell life's eternal flood.

That I might take from you
Each frightful wrenching of your frame
And make it mine instead;
That I might draw from your lips
Pain, fear, torturing fire,
And leave only love

R. Milton Carleton
Undated

Lullaby

Under my heart I carried you,
Sleep, beloved, sleep;
Night and day I felt you grow,
Sleep loved one sleep;
Now I yearned, none can know,
Sleep dearest, sleep.

R. Milton Carleton
Undated

Chicago Madonna

That frail bit of life at your breast,
Drawing from the wells of your life
The substance of being,
Brings sweet tears, and yearning
That ere another year has passed,
Neath the heart of one I love
Will lie one who is part of both of us.

Why is it that I must seek,
Ever peering oer the rim of time
Expectantly?
Is it because I feel
That neath the heart of my beloved
New life should lie?

R. Milton Carleton
Undated

Motherhood

Press deep
Soft lips upon my breast,
Press deep
To where my fulsome heart throbs sweet;
And from its beating learn
The tenderness I cannot speak.

Sing, glad heart,
And sing again,
The song that many months has
Unsung, awaiting you;
Lift again its rich refrain
Until the room is filled with love.

Close soft,
Oh trusting eyes,
Close soft
In gentle peace
And launch your tiny ship
Upon the sea of sleep.

R. Milton Carleton
Undated

Obsession

Eros
bitter antagonist,
subjecting all to bondage,
bruising with humiliation's scourge,
flaying with his barbed lash,
leaves deep-seared in living flesh…
memories.

Love,
deceptive fire,
glowing with beauty masking hate,
tempting with alluring flame,
dies, leaving only useless ash
of vain regret.

R. Milton Carleton
Undated

About the Author
Daniel Webster Carleton

Dan has been a father, a brother, a family member. His two adult children, Ace and Jordan both have followed in his footsteps and each runs his own business. Working as a machinist, a lobster fisherman, and a salesman he has managed to support himself for the last sixty years.

He taught poetry at the University of Illinois in Urbana, Illinois in the 1960's. Dan's mom, Frances Griffith Carleton encouraged him to write poetry from an early age and he never succeeded in breaking the habit.

www.ingramcontent.com/pod-product-compliance
Lightning Source LLC
Chambersburg PA
CBHW030510100426
42813CB00002B/417